# 50 Best Mexican Cheese Recipes

By: Kelly Johnson

## Table of Contents

- Queso Fundido
- Chiles Rellenos with Cheese
- Cheese Enchiladas
- Quesadilla Suprema
- Mexican Street Corn with Cotija Cheese
- Cheese and Spinach Tamales
- Chorizo and Cheese Tacos
- Mexican Cheese Dip (Queso Blanco)
- Cheese Stuffed Jalapeño Poppers
- Cheese and Mushroom Gorditas
- Three Cheese Nachos
- Mexican Cheese and Bean Empanadas
- Cheese and Potato Tacos
- Cheese-Stuffed Poblano Peppers
- Mexican Cheese Soup (Sopa de Queso)
- Cheese and Chorizo Flautas
- Mexican Cheese Pizza (Tlayuda)

- Cheese and Corn Sopes
- Cheese and Cilantro Quesadillas
- Mexican Cheese and Avocado Salad
- Cheese-Stuffed Arepas
- Cheese and Black Bean Burritos
- Cheese and Chorizo Breakfast Casserole
- Mexican Cheese and Tomato Casserole
- Cheese and Roasted Poblano Tamale Pie
- Cheese and Beef Tostadas
- Mexican Cheese-Stuffed Meatballs (Albondigas)
- Cheese and Mushroom Enchiladas
- Cheese and Chayote Casserole
- Mexican Cheese and Spinach Dip
- Cheese-Stuffed Tortilla Chips
- Cheese and Potato Chiles Toreados
- Mexican Cheese and Beef Empanadas
- Cheese and Cilantro Cornbread
- Cheese and Jalapeño Queso Blanco Dip
- Mexican Cheese-Stuffed Chicken Breasts

- Cheese and Roasted Corn Tamales
- Cheese and Chorizo Stuffed Bell Peppers
- Mexican Cheese and Bean Tacos
- Cheese and Beef Chile Rellenos
- Cheese and Mushroom Tacos
- Cheese and Tomato Enchilada Casserole
- Cheese and Cilantro Rice
- Cheese-Stuffed Chiles en Nogada
- Cheese and Black Bean Quesadillas
- Mexican Cheese and Corn Fritters
- Cheese and Roasted Vegetable Tacos
- Cheese and Jalapeño Cornbread Muffins
- Mexican Cheese and Chicken Flautas
- Cheese and Tomato Salsa Dip

## Queso Fundido

**Ingredients:**

- 2 cups shredded Oaxaca or mozzarella cheese
- ½ cup cooked chorizo or mushrooms
- 1 small onion, diced
- 1 jalapeño, minced (optional)
- Tortilla chips or warm tortillas

**Instructions:**

1. Preheat oven to 400°F (200°C).
2. In an oven-safe skillet, sauté onion and jalapeño (if using) until soft. Add cooked chorizo or mushrooms.
3. Top with shredded cheese.
4. Bake 10–15 minutes, until cheese is bubbling and lightly browned.
5. Serve hot with chips or tortillas.

**Chiles Rellenos with Cheese**

**Ingredients:**

- 4 poblano peppers
- 1½ cups shredded Monterey Jack or queso fresco
- 3 eggs, separated
- ¼ cup flour
- Oil for frying
- Tomato salsa for serving

**Instructions:**

1. Roast poblanos over open flame or broiler until skin blisters. Peel, then carefully slit and remove seeds.
2. Stuff each pepper with cheese.
3. Beat egg whites until stiff, then fold in yolks and flour.
4. Dip stuffed peppers in egg batter and fry in hot oil until golden on all sides.
5. Serve with warm tomato salsa.

**Cheese Enchiladas**

**Ingredients:**

- 8 corn tortillas
- 2 cups shredded cheese (cheddar or Mexican blend)
- 2 cups enchilada sauce
- ½ cup chopped onion
- Optional: sour cream, cilantro, jalapeños

**Instructions:**

1. Preheat oven to 375°F (190°C).
2. Lightly fry tortillas to soften.
3. Fill each with cheese and onion, roll up and place in baking dish seam-side down.
4. Cover with enchilada sauce and sprinkle more cheese on top.
5. Bake 20–25 minutes until hot and bubbly.
6. Garnish as desired.

**Quesadilla Suprema**

**Ingredients:**

- 4 large flour tortillas
- 2 cups shredded cheese (Oaxaca, mozzarella, or cheddar)
- 1 cup cooked chicken or mushrooms
- ½ cup sautéed bell peppers and onions
- Sour cream, guacamole, salsa (for serving)

**Instructions:**

1. Heat a skillet over medium.
2. Place tortilla in pan, layer with cheese, meat, and vegetables. Top with second tortilla.
3. Cook until golden, flip and cook other side.
4. Slice and serve with dips.

## Mexican Street Corn with Cotija Cheese (Elote)

**Ingredients:**

- 4 ears of corn, husked
- ¼ cup mayonnaise
- ¼ cup sour cream
- ½ cup crumbled Cotija cheese
- 1 tsp chili powder
- Juice of 1 lime

**Instructions:**

1. Grill or boil corn until cooked and lightly charred.
2. Mix mayo and sour cream; spread over corn.
3. Sprinkle with Cotija, chili powder, and lime juice.
4. Serve warm.

**Cheese and Spinach Tamales**

**Ingredients:**

- 2 cups masa harina
- 1½ cups vegetable broth
- ½ cup vegetable shortening or lard
- 1½ cups cooked spinach, chopped
- 1½ cups shredded cheese (queso fresco or Monterey Jack)
- Corn husks (soaked)

**Instructions:**

1. Mix masa, broth, and shortening into a soft dough.
2. Spread dough on corn husks, add spinach and cheese. Fold husks to close.
3. Steam tamales for 1 hour until firm.
4. Serve with salsa.

**Chorizo and Cheese Tacos**

**Ingredients:**

- 1 lb chorizo, cooked and crumbled
- 1 cup shredded cheese
- 8 small corn tortillas
- Optional toppings: onions, cilantro, avocado

**Instructions:**

1. Heat tortillas in a dry pan.
2. Fill with chorizo and sprinkle with cheese.
3. Add toppings as desired. Serve warm.

**Mexican Cheese Dip (Queso Blanco)**

**Ingredients:**

- 1 tbsp butter
- 1 small onion, minced
- 2 cups white American cheese, cubed
- ½ cup milk
- 1 jalapeño, minced (optional)
- Fresh cilantro (optional)

**Instructions:**

1. In a saucepan, melt butter and cook onion until soft.
2. Add cheese and milk, stirring until melted and smooth.
3. Stir in jalapeño and cilantro if using.
4. Serve warm with tortilla chips.

**Cheese Stuffed Jalapeño Poppers**

**Ingredients:**

- 10 fresh jalapeños
- 1 cup cream cheese
- ½ cup shredded cheddar
- ½ tsp garlic powder
- ½ tsp cumin
- Optional: bacon slices or breadcrumbs

**Instructions:**

1. Preheat oven to 400°F (200°C).
2. Halve jalapeños lengthwise and remove seeds.
3. Mix cream cheese, cheddar, garlic powder, and cumin.
4. Fill jalapeños with the mixture.
5. Optional: wrap with bacon or top with breadcrumbs.
6. Bake for 15–20 minutes until golden and bubbly.

**Cheese and Mushroom Gorditas**

**Ingredients:**

- 2 cups masa harina
- 1½ cups warm water
- 1 cup sautéed mushrooms
- 1 cup shredded Oaxaca or mozzarella cheese
- Salt to taste
- Oil for frying

**Instructions:**

1. Mix masa and water to form dough. Let rest 10 minutes.
2. Shape into small balls and flatten into thick discs.
3. Cook on a hot griddle 2–3 minutes per side.
4. Slice open one side and fill with mushrooms and cheese.
5. Return to pan or oven to melt cheese before serving.

**Three Cheese Nachos**

**Ingredients:**

- Tortilla chips
- ½ cup cheddar
- ½ cup Monterey Jack
- ½ cup queso fresco, crumbled
- ½ cup black beans
- Optional: jalapeños, salsa, sour cream, avocado

**Instructions:**

1. Preheat oven to 375°F (190°C).
2. Spread chips on a baking sheet. Top with beans and cheeses.
3. Bake for 8–10 minutes until cheese melts.
4. Top with desired garnishes and serve immediately.

**Mexican Cheese and Bean Empanadas**

**Ingredients:**

- Empanada dough or pie crust
- 1 cup refried beans
- 1 cup shredded cheese
- 1 egg (for egg wash)

**Instructions:**

1. Preheat oven to 375°F (190°C).
2. Roll out dough and cut into circles.
3. Fill each with beans and cheese. Fold and seal edges.
4. Brush with egg wash.
5. Bake for 20–25 minutes until golden.

**Cheese and Potato Tacos**

**Ingredients:**

- 2 cups diced potatoes, boiled
- 1 cup shredded cheese (cheddar or queso Oaxaca)
- ½ onion, sautéed
- Corn tortillas
- Optional toppings: salsa, sour cream, cilantro

**Instructions:**

1. Mix potatoes, cheese, and sautéed onion.
2. Fill tortillas and heat in a pan until cheese melts.
3. Serve with desired toppings.

**Cheese-Stuffed Poblano Peppers**

**Ingredients:**

- 4 poblano peppers
- 2 cups shredded cheese (Monterey Jack or Oaxaca)
- 1 tsp cumin
- 1 cup tomato sauce

**Instructions:**

1. Roast and peel poblanos.
2. Carefully stuff with cheese and cumin.
3. Place in baking dish and cover with tomato sauce.
4. Bake at 375°F (190°C) for 20–25 minutes.

**Mexican Cheese Soup (Sopa de Queso)**

**Ingredients:**

- 1 tbsp butter
- 1 small onion, chopped
- 2 cloves garlic, minced
- 2 tbsp flour
- 4 cups chicken or vegetable broth
- 1 cup milk
- 2 cups shredded cheese (cheddar, Jack, or asadero)
- Optional: diced chiles or corn

**Instructions:**

1. Sauté onion and garlic in butter.
2. Stir in flour and cook for 1–2 minutes.
3. Slowly add broth and milk. Bring to a simmer.
4. Add cheese and stir until melted.
5. Add optional ingredients and simmer 5–10 more minutes.

**Cheese and Chorizo Flautas**

**Ingredients:**

- 1 cup cooked chorizo
- 1 cup shredded cheese
- 8 small flour tortillas
- Oil for frying

**Instructions:**

1. Fill tortillas with chorizo and cheese. Roll tightly.
2. Secure with toothpicks if needed.
3. Fry in oil until golden and crispy.
4. Drain and serve with salsa or sour cream.

## Mexican Cheese Pizza (Tlayuda)

### Ingredients:

- 1 large tlayuda or flour tortilla
- ½ cup refried beans
- 1 cup shredded Oaxaca or mozzarella cheese
- ½ cup cooked chorizo or grilled veggies
- Optional: avocado, salsa, crema

### Instructions:

1. Preheat oven to 400°F (200°C).
2. Spread beans on the tlayuda.
3. Top with cheese and toppings of choice.
4. Bake 8–10 minutes or until crispy and cheese is melted.
5. Garnish with avocado or salsa.

**Cheese and Corn Sopes**

**Ingredients:**

- 2 cups masa harina
- 1½ cups warm water
- 1 cup refried beans
- 1 cup corn kernels (cooked)
- 1 cup shredded cheese (cotija or queso fresco)

**Instructions:**

1. Combine masa and water to form dough. Shape into thick discs.
2. Cook on a griddle 2–3 minutes per side. Pinch edges to form a rim.
3. Top with beans, corn, and cheese.
4. Heat briefly to melt cheese or serve warm.

**Cheese and Cilantro Quesadillas**

**Ingredients:**

- Flour or corn tortillas
- 1 cup shredded cheese (cheddar, Jack, or Oaxaca)
- ¼ cup chopped fresh cilantro
- Optional: sliced jalapeños

**Instructions:**

1. Heat a tortilla in a skillet.
2. Sprinkle cheese and cilantro over half.
3. Fold and cook until golden and cheese is melted.
4. Cut and serve with salsa or sour cream.

**Mexican Cheese and Avocado Salad**

**Ingredients:**

- 2 avocados, sliced
- ½ cup crumbled queso fresco or cotija
- 1 cup cherry tomatoes, halved
- ¼ cup red onion, thinly sliced
- Lime juice, olive oil, salt, pepper

**Instructions:**

1. Combine all ingredients in a bowl.
2. Drizzle with lime juice and olive oil.
3. Toss gently and serve immediately.

## Cheese-Stuffed Arepas

**Ingredients:**

- 2 cups pre-cooked cornmeal (masarepa)
- 1½ cups warm water
- 1 cup shredded mozzarella or queso Oaxaca
- Salt to taste
- Oil for cooking

**Instructions:**

1. Mix cornmeal, water, and salt into a dough.
2. Shape into discs and stuff with cheese.
3. Seal and flatten slightly.
4. Cook on a hot skillet until golden and cheese is melted.

**Cheese and Black Bean Burritos**

**Ingredients:**

- Flour tortillas
- 1 cup cooked black beans
- 1 cup shredded cheese
- ½ cup rice (optional)
- Salsa or sour cream

**Instructions:**

1. Warm tortillas.
2. Fill with beans, cheese, and optional rice.
3. Roll up and heat in a pan or oven until cheese melts.
4. Serve with salsa or sour cream.

**Cheese and Chorizo Breakfast Casserole**

**Ingredients:**

- 6 eggs
- ½ cup milk
- 1 cup cooked chorizo
- 1½ cups shredded cheese
- 2 cups cubed bread or tortillas
- Salt, pepper, optional veggies

**Instructions:**

1. Preheat oven to 375°F (190°C).
2. Whisk eggs, milk, salt, and pepper.
3. Combine with chorizo, cheese, and bread in a greased baking dish.
4. Bake for 30–35 minutes until set and golden.

**Mexican Cheese and Tomato Casserole**

**Ingredients:**

- 3 cups diced tomatoes (fresh or canned)
- 1½ cups shredded cheese (cheddar, queso asadero, or Jack)
- 1 cup crushed tortilla chips or cooked rice
- ½ onion, chopped
- 1 tsp cumin

**Instructions:**

1. Preheat oven to 375°F (190°C).
2. Sauté onions and combine with tomatoes, cumin, and chips/rice.
3. Layer in a baking dish with cheese.
4. Bake 20–25 minutes until bubbly.

**Cheese and Roasted Poblano Tamale Pie**

**Ingredients:**

- 1 cup cornmeal
- 1½ cups milk
- 2 roasted poblanos, peeled and chopped
- 1 cup shredded cheese (cheddar, Jack, or Oaxaca)
- ½ tsp cumin, salt to taste
- 1 egg (optional, for richness)

**Instructions:**

1. Preheat oven to 375°F (190°C).
2. Simmer milk and whisk in cornmeal, stirring until thick.
3. Mix in poblanos, cheese, spices, and egg.
4. Pour into a greased baking dish and bake for 25–30 minutes until set.

**Cheese and Beef Tostadas**

**Ingredients:**

- Tostada shells
- 1 cup cooked ground beef (with taco seasoning)
- 1 cup shredded cheese
- Lettuce, salsa, sour cream, avocado

**Instructions:**

1. Layer beef on tostadas.
2. Top with cheese and melt under a broiler (optional).
3. Add fresh toppings and serve immediately.

## Mexican Cheese-Stuffed Meatballs (Albondigas)

**Ingredients:**

- 1 lb ground beef
- ½ cup breadcrumbs
- 1 egg
- 1 tsp cumin, salt, pepper
- Small cubes of queso fresco or mozzarella

**Instructions:**

1. Mix beef, breadcrumbs, egg, and seasoning.
2. Form meatballs around a cube of cheese.
3. Bake at 375°F (190°C) for 20–25 minutes or simmer in tomato sauce.

**Cheese and Mushroom Enchiladas**

**Ingredients:**

- Corn tortillas
- 1 cup sautéed mushrooms
- 1½ cups shredded cheese
- 1½ cups enchilada sauce

**Instructions:**

1. Fill tortillas with mushrooms and cheese, roll up.
2. Place in a baking dish, top with enchilada sauce and more cheese.
3. Bake at 375°F (190°C) for 20 minutes.

**Cheese and Chayote Casserole**

**Ingredients:**

- 2–3 chayotes, peeled and sliced thin
- 1 cup shredded cheese (cheddar or Jack)
- ½ cup crema or sour cream
- ¼ cup chopped onion
- Salt, pepper

**Instructions:**

1. Preheat oven to 375°F (190°C).
2. Layer chayote slices with cheese, onions, and crema.
3. Bake for 30–35 minutes until bubbly and tender.

**Mexican Cheese and Spinach Dip**

**Ingredients:**

- 1 cup cooked spinach (drained)
- 1 cup cream cheese
- ½ cup sour cream
- 1 cup shredded cheese (Mexican blend)
- Garlic, cumin, salt

**Instructions:**

1. Mix all ingredients in a bowl.
2. Bake at 350°F (175°C) for 20 minutes or microwave until hot and melted.
3. Serve with tortilla chips.

**Cheese-Stuffed Tortilla Chips**

**Ingredients:**

- Corn tortillas
- Shredded cheese (cheddar or queso Oaxaca)
- Oil for frying

**Instructions:**

1. Cut tortillas into triangles and sandwich cheese between two.
2. Fry until golden and cheese is melted.
3. Drain on paper towels and serve warm.

**Cheese and Potato Chiles Toreados**

**Ingredients:**

- 4 jalapeños or serrano chiles, blistered in a pan
- ½ cup mashed potatoes
- ½ cup shredded cheese
- Salt to taste

**Instructions:**

1. Slit roasted chiles and remove seeds if desired.
2. Mix potatoes and cheese, stuff into chiles.
3. Warm in a skillet or bake until cheese melts.

## Mexican Cheese and Beef Empanadas

### Ingredients:

- Empanada dough or pastry rounds
- 1 cup cooked ground beef (seasoned)
- 1 cup shredded cheese (cheddar, Oaxaca, or Monterey Jack)
- 1 egg (for egg wash)

### Instructions:

1. Preheat oven to 375°F (190°C).
2. Place a spoonful of beef and cheese in each dough round.
3. Fold and seal with a fork; brush with egg wash.
4. Bake for 20–25 minutes until golden.

## Cheese and Cilantro Cornbread

**Ingredients:**

- 1 cup cornmeal
- 1 cup flour
- 1 tbsp baking powder
- 1 cup milk
- 1 egg
- 1 cup shredded cheese
- ¼ cup chopped cilantro
- Salt, optional jalapeños

**Instructions:**

1. Preheat oven to 375°F (190°C).
2. Mix dry ingredients, then stir in milk, egg, cheese, and cilantro.
3. Pour into greased pan, bake for 25–30 minutes.

# Cheese and Jalapeño Queso Blanco Dip

**Ingredients:**

- 1 tbsp butter
- 1 tbsp flour
- 1 cup milk
- 2 cups white American cheese or Monterey Jack, shredded
- 1 jalapeño, finely chopped

**Instructions:**

1. Melt butter, stir in flour to make a roux.
2. Slowly add milk, then stir in cheese until melted.
3. Add jalapeños, simmer until thick. Serve warm.

**Mexican Cheese-Stuffed Chicken Breasts**

**Ingredients:**

- 2 chicken breasts
- ½ cup shredded cheese
- 1 tsp cumin, garlic powder
- Salt, pepper

**Instructions:**

1. Slice a pocket in each chicken breast.
2. Fill with cheese, season, and secure with toothpicks.
3. Sear and bake at 375°F (190°C) for 20–25 minutes.

**Cheese and Roasted Corn Tamales**

**Ingredients:**

- 2 cups masa harina
- 1½ cups broth
- 1/3 cup lard or shortening
- 1 cup roasted corn
- 1 cup shredded cheese
- Corn husks, soaked

**Instructions:**

1. Mix masa, broth, and lard until smooth.
2. Spread on husks, fill with corn and cheese.
3. Fold and steam for 1–1½ hours until firm.

**Cheese and Chorizo Stuffed Bell Peppers**

**Ingredients:**

- 4 bell peppers, halved and seeded
- 1 cup cooked chorizo
- 1 cup shredded cheese
- ½ cup cooked rice (optional)

**Instructions:**

1. Preheat oven to 375°F (190°C).
2. Mix chorizo, cheese, and rice. Stuff into peppers.
3. Bake for 25–30 minutes.

**Mexican Cheese and Bean Tacos**

**Ingredients:**

- Corn tortillas
- 1 cup refried beans
- 1 cup shredded cheese
- Lettuce, salsa, avocado

**Instructions:**

1. Heat tortillas, spread with beans and sprinkle cheese.
2. Add toppings and serve immediately.

**Cheese and Beef Chile Rellenos**

**Ingredients:**

- 4 poblano peppers, roasted and peeled
- 1 cup cooked ground beef
- 1 cup shredded cheese
- 2 eggs, separated
- 2 tbsp flour
- Oil for frying

**Instructions:**

1. Stuff poblanos with beef and cheese.
2. Whip egg whites, fold in yolks and flour.
3. Dip chiles in batter and fry until golden.

**Cheese and Mushroom Tacos**

**Ingredients:**

- Corn tortillas
- 2 cups mushrooms, sliced
- 1 cup shredded cheese (Oaxaca or Monterey Jack)
- 1 clove garlic, minced
- 1 tbsp olive oil
- Salt and pepper to taste

**Instructions:**

1. Sauté mushrooms with garlic in olive oil until tender. Season with salt and pepper.
2. Warm tortillas, add sautéed mushrooms and cheese.
3. Fold and heat until cheese melts. Serve hot.

**Cheese and Tomato Enchilada Casserole**

**Ingredients:**

- 8 corn tortillas, torn
- 2 cups shredded cheese
- 2 cups tomato sauce
- ½ cup chopped onions
- 1 tsp cumin

**Instructions:**

1. Preheat oven to 375°F (190°C).
2. Layer tortillas, sauce, cheese, and onions in a baking dish.
3. Repeat layers and finish with cheese on top.
4. Bake for 25–30 minutes until bubbly and golden.

**Cheese and Cilantro Rice**

**Ingredients:**

- 1 cup cooked white rice
- ½ cup shredded cheese (cheddar or Cotija)
- ¼ cup chopped cilantro
- Juice of ½ lime
- Salt to taste

**Instructions:**

1. Mix hot rice with cheese until melted.
2. Stir in cilantro, lime juice, and salt.
3. Serve warm as a side or taco filling.

## Cheese-Stuffed Chiles en Nogada

**Ingredients:**

- 4 poblano peppers, roasted and peeled
- 1 cup queso fresco or Monterey Jack
- ½ cup chopped nuts (optional)
- 1 cup walnut cream sauce (blend soaked walnuts, milk, a bit of sugar and cinnamon)
- Pomegranate seeds and parsley for garnish

**Instructions:**

1. Stuff chiles with cheese and nuts (if using).
2. Place on a plate and spoon over walnut sauce.
3. Garnish with pomegranate seeds and parsley.

**Cheese and Black Bean Quesadillas**

**Ingredients:**

- Flour tortillas
- 1 cup black beans (cooked or canned)
- 1 cup shredded cheese
- ½ tsp chili powder

**Instructions:**

1. Mash beans lightly with chili powder.
2. Spread beans and cheese on a tortilla, top with another.
3. Grill in a pan until golden and cheese melts. Cut into wedges.

## Mexican Cheese and Corn Fritters

**Ingredients:**

- 1 cup corn kernels
- ½ cup shredded cheese
- ½ cup flour
- 1 egg
- ¼ cup chopped scallions
- Salt and pepper
- Oil for frying

**Instructions:**

1. Mix corn, cheese, flour, egg, scallions, salt, and pepper.
2. Heat oil in a pan. Drop spoonfuls of batter and flatten slightly.
3. Fry until golden brown on both sides. Drain and serve warm.

**Cheese and Roasted Vegetable Tacos**

**Ingredients:**

- Corn tortillas
- 1 zucchini, diced
- 1 bell pepper, diced
- 1 small red onion, sliced
- 1 tbsp olive oil
- 1 cup shredded cheese (Oaxaca, Monterey Jack, or cheddar)
- Salt, pepper, cumin to taste

**Instructions:**

1. Preheat oven to 425°F (220°C). Toss vegetables with olive oil and spices, spread on a baking sheet, and roast for 20–25 minutes.
2. Warm tortillas, fill with roasted vegetables and cheese.
3. Serve with salsa or avocado if desired.

# Cheese and Jalapeño Cornbread Muffins

**Ingredients:**

- 1 cup cornmeal
- 1 cup flour
- 1 tbsp baking powder
- 1 cup milk
- 1 egg
- 1 cup shredded cheddar cheese
- 1 jalapeño, finely chopped
- ¼ cup melted butter

**Instructions:**

1. Preheat oven to 375°F (190°C). Grease or line a muffin tin.
2. In a bowl, mix dry ingredients. In another bowl, mix wet ingredients. Combine both.
3. Fold in cheese and jalapeño.
4. Spoon into muffin tin and bake 18–22 minutes.

## Mexican Cheese and Chicken Flautas

**Ingredients:**

- 2 cups shredded cooked chicken
- 1 cup shredded cheese (cheddar, Monterey Jack, or blend)
- 8 small flour tortillas
- Oil for frying or brushing
- Salsa and sour cream for serving

**Instructions:**

1. Mix chicken and cheese. Place a few tablespoons on each tortilla and roll tightly.
2. Fry in oil until golden and crispy or bake at 400°F (200°C) for 15–20 minutes.
3. Serve with salsa and sour cream.

**Cheese and Tomato Salsa Dip**

**Ingredients:**

- 1 cup diced tomatoes (fresh or canned, drained)
- 1 clove garlic, minced
- 1 cup shredded cheese (cheddar or Mexican blend)
- ¼ cup chopped onions
- 1 tbsp olive oil
- Salt and chili flakes to taste

**Instructions:**

1. In a skillet, sauté onions and garlic in olive oil.
2. Add tomatoes, salt, and chili flakes. Simmer 5 minutes.
3. Stir in cheese until melted and creamy.
4. Serve warm with tortilla chips.